Verses of Miscellany

Verses of Miscellany

Viti Uttreja

PAPER TOWNS
PUBLISHERS

First Published by
Paper Towns Publishers
72, Vishwanath Dham Colony,
Niwaru Road, Jhotwara,
Jaipur, 302012

Verses of Miscellany

ISBN Print Book - 978-93-6185-905-2

Printed in India

for the ones

who like to dwell

into the deep well

of their imaginative soul

CONTENTS

3. THE EVER-CHANGING VERDANT BEAUTY

-The Crimson Flames of Passion

-The Calm Before the Storm

-The Gift of Nature

4. SOCIETY

-Useless Globules that are a Method to Cope with Life

-Distractions

-Pal

5. THE FAITHFUL ALLEGIANCE

-Unite as One

-Crest of Freedom

6. THE UNDENIABLE TRUTH

-True Purpose

Disenchanted

Love

Unfulfilled Promises

Tangled up in a mess
More complicated than a game of chess,
Had given my all,
Without expecting anything in return.

Minutes turned into hours,
I still remember the flowers
That you gave on the first day
Holding my hand with a sweet gesture.

Hours turned into days,
You had become my sunshine's rays.
Your voice grew into my daily routine,
Such soft, gentle words, all directed towards me.

Days turned into months,
Our relationship took off to lengths,
We commemorated and celebrated
Promised to always have each other's backs.

Suddenly one day you moved away,
During the hot summery month of May.
Tried to keep in contact but lost touch
Was this how it all ended?

Bidding Goodbye to my Feelings, With a Smile Plastered on my face

With a deep desire in my heart,
I wished you to be mine.
But as I bid you goodbye that day,
A broken heart, yet a smile plastered on my face.

Somehow fate had us cross our paths,
We met as old lovers
Yet once again,
My heart continued to beat for you.

Things remained the same,
You got a lover while I felt like a substitute
Silently crying as I supported you everyday,
With a smile plastered on my face.

People call one plastic with a fake personality,
But I guess I was plastic for protecting my feelings.
My heart burnt to ashes,
As I saw you two walking with your hands
interlocked, happiness radiating from your faces.

I expressed happiness for you the best I could,
Even as my soul seemed to perish
Yet I continued with the misery
With a smile plastered on my face.

It was the end of spring,
Your love bloomed under the cherry blossoms,
While I was left alone
Remaining your friend for that's all I could.

A Stab In The Heart

Dancing in the meadows
Outside your house in the daylight,
As we threw away our crazy stilettos
Felt as if we took our first flight,
Towards not caring
About what others had to say.

As I thought about those days
Sipping coffee while looking outside my window
Thinking about how I watched you in all those plays,
How you ran towards me whenever I experienced vertigo,
How we guaranteed to meet even after school ended,
All those promises made that we couldn't fulfill.

Those memories turned into daydreams,
Now I led my monotonous, mediocre life silently
Everyday living in the absence of your eminent gleams,
As you kept me in the dark about your anxiety.
Getting to know through others about the disdain you committed felt like a stab in the heart,
Why did you decide to end it all, my dear friend?

Catalysts of Encouragement

Take the Lead

There's one who leads,
And one who follows.
Seemingly, a small difference between the two
Yet a big effect that follows.

It all depends upon one's nature,
That decides their future.
Going an extra mile,
Or taking it easy in the present.

Not through sinful means,
But through good deeds
Be someone others look upto,
Not one others look down on.

Determination and courage drives you on,
To achieve success in life bang on.
The one who takes the lead is remembered,
While the one who follows remains silently buried.

Choose the path that is right,
Not the path that is easy.
Either be remembered as a leader,
Or fade away with time as a follower.

Brave Little Souls

Swept across the field,
The brave little souls soar through
going past the countless yield,
Looking at the sky into which they flew.

As one man gazes past the hazy sun,
The dandelion seeds dance in the wind.
One might assume they have fun,
But these brave little souls have a journey
one of a kind.

Their expedition is a long, harsh path
because of which many fail.
But hold it, this is just nature's wrath,
And the brave little souls who complete their voyage are the ones who sail.

It is a world of survival out there,
Everyone looks out to make themselves the best.
Not all can in a world that is a facade of fair,
But the brave little souls who make it are the ones who break it, and grow into a beautiful flower with their own little crest.

The Strength to Resist

Courage gives one ways
to pave their path,
Even on the hardest of days,
In the difficult times of man's wrath.

Resistance drives one forward,
Even when the times are grim.
Doesn't matter if they were once sheltered
in the leeward,
The will to survive and resist pulls them
through even when the days are dim.

Unexpected events occur with one another,
All one needs is the strength to resist.
It gives upliftment like none other
Even when the burdensome period persist.

Pure courage can make one go lengths,
Whether to survive or to thrive
As long as one has the strengths.

The Ever-Changing Verdant Beauty

The Crimson Flames of Passion

It sets ablaze everything it touches,
With a loud crackle as it burns.
It spreads its orange wings,
Pride dripping from it's flames.

People fear it with their lives,
As it beckons it's call of destruction
bringing loss to the countless families
with it's crimson wings spread wide.

Strong fires flourish in the wind,
Fueled with strength
as they become one with it,
The cunning little one grows.

The one who tears it apart becomes the hero,
But even with its weakness out in the open,
it continues to spread its passion,
Set to conquer and burn everything it sets its eyes on.

The Calm Before the Storm

The rage of thunder,
Is surely not a blunder.
Doesn't come at its own,
As lightning follows its tone.

This is the storm,
Calamity in its strongest form.
But there is always a warning,
Without an actual mourning.

Where flowers bloom,
There they gloom
Still like gentle trees,
As it eventually turns into a shrewd breeze.

It always comes with a warning
just like the moon waning.
Day by day, the brightness short,
Oh reader, this is the calm before the storm.

The Gift of Nature

As beautiful as flowers in daylight,
As peaceful as the moon at night,
As serene as water enveloped in mist,
As appealing as the sunset before dusk.

The bestowal from nature is priceless,
It is absolute, it is timeless.
But by the misconduct of human deeds,
The perennial creation decays with the passage of time.

Come together on this day,
Start small, but start away,
Undo the felonies upon nature
Before it all collapses into demise.

Society

Useless Globules that are a Method to Cope with Life

Tears and raindrops, all of them fall,
Mostly the result of physical, chemical or
emotional brawl.
Feared by many, the way of life for other
Yet perceived by all as a bother.

They patter on the surfaces which they drop,
One accompanied by other, as they fall on top.
Carry around lots of emotions in small globules,
Many of which are sequels of squabbles.

Discerned as 'useless' by a lot of people,
Judged that it makes them feeble.
But sometimes, tears give one the strength to face the actuality,
All it relies on is one's mentality.

Yet, they aren't 'wrong', after all are the result of our emotions,
Whether they're joyous or from corrosions.
Just, don't judge the sensitive crowd,
They've got enough on their plates endowed.

Distractions

The wind spits and smithers in my face,
A tall wall looms in front of me
blocking me off from ameliorating,
All in the midst of midnight.

A dog gently closes his eyes and rests his chin on his paws.
In the silence of midnight,
echoes the ball as it levitates in different directions.
A strange, buttery smell lurks in the air.

A miss, a hit, yet again a miss.
The wall in front obstructs me from the pure bliss
of hitting the ball again and again,
All in the midst of midnight.

Pal

Friends are a treasure of gold,
The connection with whom never gets old.
Friends are like the bright fireflies in the darkness,
Bringing in light even when the times are filled with distress.

Cherishable moments with them never pass away,
Get the friends who never let you go astray.
Because behind every successful person also lies a friend,
Oh my dear reader, dis du comprehend.

Even when one lies conflicted,
A friend stops you from being inflicted.
Find the friends who support you to go to the just path,
not the ones who leave you scath.

The Faithful Allegiance

Unite as One

War is never the solution,
All it brings is demolition.
Harmony exists in the times of peace,
Friendships begin when enemies call a truce.

Throw apart the differences that everyone hath,
Because war leaves all scath.
We all bleed the same colour,
Let humanity unite as one
Why discolour?

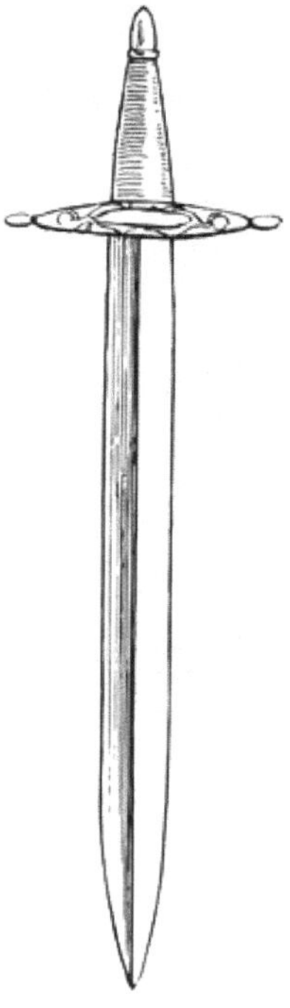

The Crest of Freedom

Where the words "Our Nation" ring in one's ears,
The heart sings with pride and tears.
Belongingness bestows solace to the psyche like
none other,
Whither all croon carefree, "This is our mother!"

The burning fire of faith and fervency favour the
realm,
To go above and beyond to dishelm
The haven of other that once rested in the leeward,
With unity altogether they forge forward.

Is that very much the true patriotism we all desire?
Or just humanity's greed to ascend higher?
From a well of pious angelic love it emerged,
Wherefore removed it to unfold purged?

The crape myrtle of untainted agape,
Shimmers in the dusk even as darkness drape.
As the creek continues to ripple and zephyr rise,
The emblem of freedom soars to the skies.

The Undeniable Truth

True Purpose

People go lengths to achieve success,
Go to work everyday and earn money,
Support their families for goodwill sakes,
But has anyone stopped to give a thought?

Why do we live this life?
Do we all have a particular purpose upon this
Earth?
Why were we created by God in the first place,
who even are we truly?
If not, why do we even play along?

No, everyone blindly follows the system
without questioning their true purpose,
Goes off to 'contribute' to the 'society and
humanity'
Creates their own system of belief and faith.

Those who deviate from this system are condemned down to "get back to their senses"
And become sheep again who blindly follow the crowd, without ever having an idea of where they are led to.

We are mere playthings in this universe,
who created societies and communities as a pastime.
Thinking we're almighty and of utmost importance
But no, we will never understand the true purpose of our existence.

Neither will we ever understand the purpose of creation of life and the world around,
So the only thing that matters is questioning our own beliefs. What are we doing, to us and to everybody around us, if it is the right thing to do?
And, what really is the "right thing" to do in this mere, small world of ours?

Gratitude is a form of expression that makes people feel loved.

Acknowledgement

I really liked writing the array of poems in this book. Even sometimes as I struggled with new topics, thanks to the constant support and eagerness of my family and friends, I was able to pen down my imaginations and come up with my first collection of poems. I hope you enjoyed reading these as much as I enjoyed writing them!

I thank my parents, especially my mother for supporting me in writing this book however possible.

I would also like to express gratitude to my grandparents, the support of whom meant a lot. Another thank you, to my late grandpa for always motivating me and being there for me.

Lastly, a special thanks to all my friends who helped me out whenever I needed it.

A poem is a message of expression of the mind,

the heart, the soul and the body.

ABOUT THE AUTHOR

Viti is a young, self-publishing author, venturing in the abstract field of poetry. With a strong imagination combined with a love for movies of all genres, her poems cover a large number of topics from the pain of a broken heart to the beauties of nature all around. She is a keen writer, who enjoys reading poems and understanding the point of views of other authors alongside her own.